All the Things She Thinks About

April Snyder

BookLeaf Publishing

Presentation by *BookLeaf Publishing*

Web: www.bookleafpub.com

E-mail: info@bookleafpub.com

ISBN: 9789358738483

First edition 2023

*I dedicate this book to my late mother,
Gloria. You were and still are an
inspiration to me. You have always
encouraged me to be creative, and to be my
best self. I love you and miss you so much.
This body of work is for you.*

ACKNOWLEDGEMENT

I would first like to thank God. I know this talent comes from you, and that's why the desire to write burns so bright. I hope to honor you with this gift! Thank you to everyone who has ever encouraged me to write. I keep writing because you push me to continue, even when I have doubted myself. I would like to thank Ben Snyder Jr., Ben Snyder Sr., Meaghan McBee, Jennifer Corley, Jessi Hersey, Pastor Breanne Stewart, Thomas and Will. Your support means a lot to me.

Leadership Philosophy

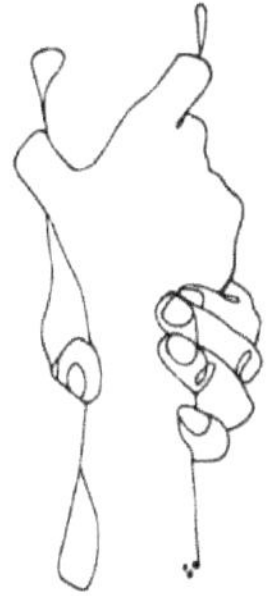

Leadership is about service
Making myself available to you
Whenever there is a problem
We will work it through

Whenever the workload is heavy
I will roll my sleeves up
You're not alone on this journey
I will always show up

Safe spaces will be provided to all
Everyone will be included in decisions
Even when we fall
We will all rise with precision

There will be times that we come to yes
But sometimes decisions will lead to a no
We will discuss things together

Our conclusion we will sow

Empathy is the call I will answer
To value people is to plant a seed
Leadership is nothing without a team
Diverse perceptions are what we need

It will be my duty to protect all
That I've been chosen to guide
You'll always be heard
Your confidence I will hide

We'll treat each other with dignity
I will always have your back
No under bus trickery
No personal attacks

There are days I may have to call you out
But I rather call you in
This will be a place to welcome all
We'll reside within the quadrant den

I'll always analyze and manage self
Be sure to be socially aware
I'll use relationship management
To encourage potential leaders with care

Leaders should inspire others
To advance with integrity

Your actions and words
Will be what they believe and see

We will learn and collaborate together
Communicate our ideas and goals
Make plans and forecast success
Plan strategies and identify roles

I will take responsibility when we fail
Fairly manage conflicts we come across
Be resilient through it all
Receiving constructive feedback is never a loss

My leadership philosophy
Will be that we help each other grow
Value and raise each other
To build a legacy and not a show

You Will Not Fail

So much smaller when you're young
But mountains get larger as you grow
Challenges surround you like a flood
Or they freeze you like the snow

We drown in overthinking
Questioning our place in time
Falling like an anchor sinking
Fretting the shifts in our paradigm

Change in the slightest thing
Raises our potential phobia
Pushing our mind to swing
In the direction of our doubts

Pull the daisies up
Where you buried your strength
Fill the other half of your cup
With courage and fullness

Talk yourself into ableness
As you did with your fear
Talk yourself into capable
Let it sauté in your mind and seer

You can do it all
The light can now see you
You will not fail
Success for you is due

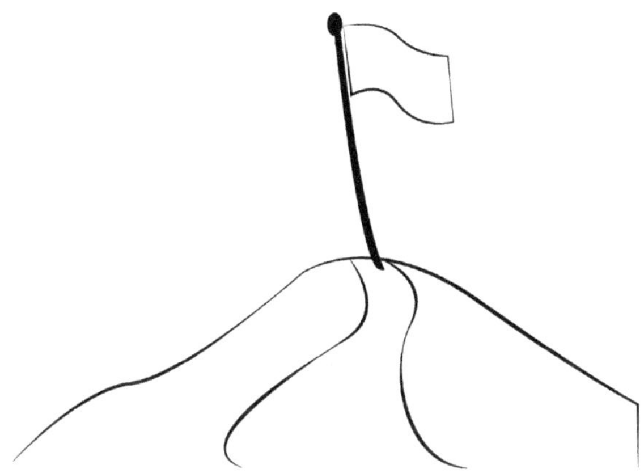

Purpose Searching

We're all here for a purpose
At first the reason unclear
We have to pursue that purpose
We have to do it without fear

Some know it from the start
Others are still searching
People are looking in their heart
For the talent given to them by You

I know You made us for a reason
You put us on earth to do something special
Now is our season
To do the work You built in us

I pray that everyday
I make You proud
Let the words that I write
Pierce through the clouds

May these words bring You glory
May they help change lives
When I write a story
I want to encourage people to strive

To be true to themselves
Find the voice deep within
You created them for a reason
You created them to win

To everyone looking
May you find out why you're here
Your existence is meaningful
That much should be clear

Never cease to pray
Find out what's inside
May you share it with the world
In whatever way God decides

Empathy

Some people can relate and feel the pain of another

Most experience and can understand if

People used the dots to connect their hearts

Amplify their souls toward humankind

There are endless opportunities to relate and

Help one another by understanding that

You can see their pain

Informal Ignorance

Amazed by the ones that willfully
Look away from actual information
To fulfill a narrative they created
To feed their imagination
Forsaking the knowledge
That will save them from drowning
In the pool of nonsense
Created by the person
That has a brain but
Uses it to disseminate division
In order to meet the goal
Of turning people against
Their own interests
Because misinformation
Has drawn their brains
To one source

Fight the love of ignorance
Surround yourselves with all
Information giving life to your thoughts
Using discernment to follow
The truth about the globe
You inhabit by fighting the
Desire to be monogamous
To a toxic relationship

Bent on whispering disinformation
To your thoughts
Tinkering with your soul
To anger you over
Conspiracies created by the bitter

Heart Heavy

I can't carry it anymore
These unsaid words
Mounting like anvils
Upon my chest
Staggering my breathing
As the pain dances around
Until I discover relief
In pen and paper
Between the college ruled lines
Fingers dancing on the keyboard
Letting my soul bleed out
Through words
Releasing the anguish
Like a wave pushing the residue

From the crowded sea
Unto the shore
Instantly lifting the pressure
Giving my heart permission
To be free of my worries and pain

Slate

13

Snow blankets the earth
Extract summer's leftovers
Renews the surface

Lessons After Walking

We knew it was time for a walk
When your cane was in your hand
We paced ourselves to get ready
To stroll through the neighborhood
It energized us and calmed us down
So that when we arrived back home
We didn't make a sound
Prayer, breakfast and a lesson were in store
It was time for wisdom
She was knowledgeable to her core
Some lessons were visible to our eyes
Others were explained to us
We got through the lows and the highs
The nonverbal but verbal lessons
Were to pray, read the word and devotions
She did this everyday
Grandma was holiness in motion
We were taught to love
Even when we didn't like
We knew that only God from above
Sent us Grandma's light
She encouraged us to speak to people
Even when we didn't want to say hello
When she felt weak
Her strength was on the go

She taught us to give
We inherited that from her
She taught us to live
From that we did infer
It all started with our walks
Learning our faithful lessons
I miss her talks
Our learning sessions

Black Sheep Mentality

I'm the one they talk about as
They put their hands up
Over their faces when they see me

The rumors they heard are key
To their behavior
I'm the black sheep

The one that did something wrong
Listen to them sing the song
About how I failed in an area
Of my life that I didn't

But family knows
Because cousin so and so
Revealed the so-called truth
That I have no couth

When it comes to other family
Uncle such and such
Knows a little too much
Of absolutely nothing

Because his truth is false
And projecting is his mission

So that you could make your decision
About the black sheep

Removing the eyes off
Your own deceit
Using the devil's technique
And his brew of division and defeat

As this is the way you become
The star of your own story
While the sheep is abandoned
By those who think they know
The truth without a doubt

If only they knew
That this sheep is not the cause
Of the pain you said I inflicted
But the one you inflicted
The pain upon

I will wear my black sheep status
Proudly because God knows
Even if those here on earth
Have accepted your words as fact
And turned their backs on me
For life until eternity

That I am not who you say I am
I am who God says I am

And the truth will reveal itself
On the day you have to
Answer for your words

Until then I will wear
This dark wool with a smile

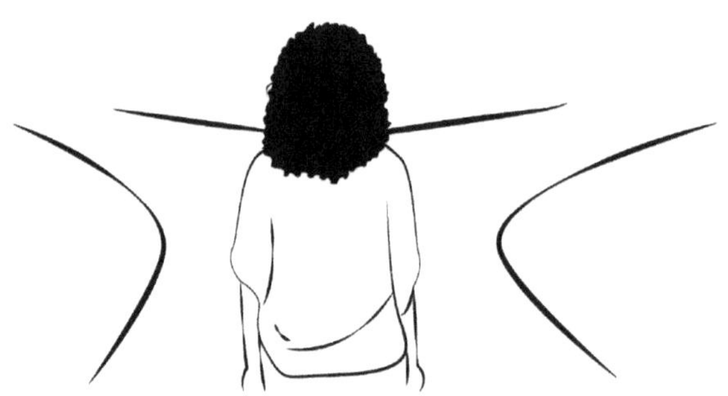

Just Start

Procrastination and doubt
Prevent us from starting
The pursuit of our passions
Sure we talk about it
We even think about it
There are even dreams
That soak within our psyche
But we put it on hold
We are afraid of our ability to try
We are unsure of our ability to be successful

Fear should be as easy to lose
As our keys to our homes and cars
Our ability to propel in our field
As easy as pushing the add to cart button
On that delicious purchase

That we shouldn't buy
Give in to the passion
That surrounds your soul
Stand up in your purpose
And just start

Dear Mom

You always showed us love
Genuine kindness and care
I never thought that one day
You wouldn't be there

As a child I used to think
My family would live forever
Death was never an option
Life would be a continuous endeavor

First grandfather left this world
My grandmother years after
Other relatives took leave of earth
We missed their presence in our next chapter

With age and maturity
My delusions of immortality faded
Then you left this world

And my view became jaded

We miss your voice
Your smile your laugh
We miss our mom
Our whole hearts now in half

I miss our chats
We discussed everything
I miss your prayers
I miss hearing you sing

You were our defender
You are in our heart
We were devastated
When it was time to depart

This grief is unbearable
It hurts our souls
We cry at any moment
We just don't feel whole

We know you are in heaven
Spreading all the joy
Trading songs with angels
Not missing earth's noise

When it's our time to leave
We hope to see you there

Save a space beside you
We'll be waiting on heaven's stair

23

Fairytale of the Heart

The heart of the single woman
May have changed over time
Singleness is fine with some
But love is still on several minds

Social media is flooded
With endless couples' goals
Rose petals and candle proposals
Leaving our hearts to lose control

Some of us still dream
That we will find the perfect man
That love will find us
Childhood fairytales will stand

We want that romantic ending
The ones you see in movies
He shows up at that perfect moment
In love you fall truly

Reality deals heavy blows
The longer the lovelorn stay single
You start to lose hope
Your plans develop wrinkles

I had a timeline
A good and honest plan
I would get a job out of college
And then I would find my man

Time flew by like a bird
And not a single thing
Came true like I thought
I had work but still no king

Desire for love suffocated me
As the years withered by
I learned to enjoy my own company
At least I would try

Use your single time
To love who you are
Fall in love with your purpose
Shine with that as your star

Still I hold on to that fairytale
For love to come and be
I will cherish myself
Until he finds me

Free Flying Spirit

Sometimes your spirit feels trapped
In a job that pulls on your soul
Taking everything out of you
Delaying your goals

There has to be something freeing
About following your passion and dreams
Some make it look easy
For others it's harder than it seems

Don't let your unhappiness trap you
In a constant roundabout
Of the strenuous day to day
There is always a way out

Pursue the rope around your heart
Attacking your lack of belief
In yourself is the very passion
Saving yourself from unnecessary grief

You don't have to spend years in the same place
Work on the thing your heart tells you to do
Make time in between the grind
Let your spirit begin anew

Leading Sunlight

Sunlit grass path soaked
In possibilities and opportunities
Leads to a marvelous peace
Found only in joy

Start The Day

The birds get up and start to sing
Before my phone lets out a ring
That's when I start to cry
About the night flying by

A good and cold autumn day
Encourages the late morning stay
In endless thread count sheets
Listening to the cars roll on the streets

I really hate to tell my pillow goodbye
It's enough to take a breath, breathe and sigh
It's the thought of having to do it all over again
Realizing today is the day and not then

It's time to run the hamster wheel
And film the life journey reel
Of how I usually start my day
By moving my body from where I lay

I find the will to finally move
Put on a song to help me groove
And take the steps to go to work
There are no duties that I will shirk

I will give this day my very best
Pass any struggles and beat the test
I have the capability to do so
I just have to get up and go

I Write

I write to release the pain
Release the grief
Attempt to stay sane
And lean on my belief

I write to pour
The heaviness from my heart
In order to soar
And pierce the air like a dart

I write because I'm compelled
My voice aches to be heard
My destiny is spelled
My vision never blurred

I write to help people
Who need to be encouraged
To stop every evil
And gain all their courage

Pen and paper are the tools I love
Exercising them is all I need
Writing is a gift from above
This calling I will heed

I'll write in the day
I'll write in the night
I'll say all that I have to say
I'll write, I'll write, I'll write

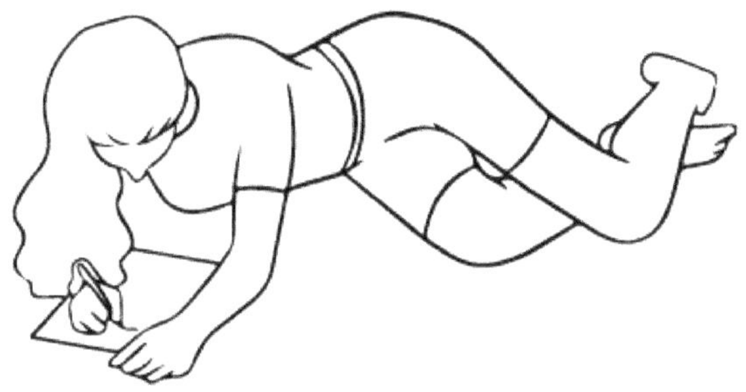

Dear April

Dear April of the future
Wherever you may be
You made it further than you thought
You saw all that you could see

You met many people
That you thought you would never meet
But you lost some loved ones
That your heart still keeps

You had many interesting moments
You went through some tests
You found all your missing components
You had times that you couldn't rest

You made mistakes
That you lived over and over again
Overthinking made
You relive your worst sins

You had difficulty letting go of the past
It was hard finding your way
You never thought you would last
To hear what I have to say

You are at your best point in life
There is nothing you can't do
You suffered through all the strife
You believed in you
There is still more to see
More reasons for you to smile
I wish that life could let you be
But it may not be for awhile

You will still go through things
But you will be okay
Lay on your angel's wing
You will make it another day

Make It To The Paper

Hastily running to find a pen
And diving for that one paper slither
In the most impossible spot
As the words dance around
Until it forms insightful thoughts
Into small statements
Line by line to create
The poem you've held
In your mind and heart most of the day
Racing to write it down
Or scramble to your laptop
Before what materializes
Disappears and the search for ideas
And perfect flow of words
Begins again
Trying to muster

That same perfection of streaming words
To release the poem
That you ache to bring to life

Void of Humanity

It saddens me to see
The lack of humanity
In humankind
Some of it is still there
But some have lost their mind

The lack of empathy
Gives me pause
How do you give up
On your fellow human
How do you just not care
There is someone that needs you
They are standing right there

Where is the compassion
That I once saw

People cared for one another
Now they fight, bite and claw
At each other over the simplest things
Fighting over things that don't matter
Fighting where there is no fight to be had
It grieves my flabbergasted heart
It makes me sad

Step into the shoes
Of the one you judge
Take the time to evaluate and choose
Your reaction carefully
Are you hearing me

The lack of love and understanding
Is blinding you to your behavior
And crippling your fellow person
While they fight their battle
And stand alone under the sun

Discover your empathy again
Regain your humanity
Reach for your compassion
Because you never know
When you will need it
From the same human
You denied it to

The Writing Introvert

There is energy in quiet
Void of noise
Distant from the endless talking
Of overzealous extroverts
With a gift of gab
That would put an auctioneer to shame
My ears are no longer overwhelmed
By the constant ringing arrangement
Pertaining to the contribution
Of any object with the ability
To cause a crazy commotion
My favorite is hearing
Absolutely nothing
As it inspires me
To complete my recent challenge
Writing poetry day by day

Explaining all I have to say
Using all the words rumbling
Through my mind
In a short amount of time
To create a lasting book
Of various thoughts and ideas

Journey of Purpose

I have given you all I have
Said what I needed to say
This is my word journey
The sunset to my day

I gave in to a challenge
It tested the strength of my pen
There is still room for me to grow
This beginning is not my end

I relinquish this gift to God
May He give it light
Use these words to heal and help
Invoke passion and ignite

There is a purpose in each of you
It's aching to get out
Sometimes it takes a challenge
To eliminate your doubt

We often don't believe enough
To share what is inside
We usually need reassurance
We hoard our gifts and hide

It's scary to actually try
To give life a purpose
But if we give it all we have
We'll find it's truly worth it

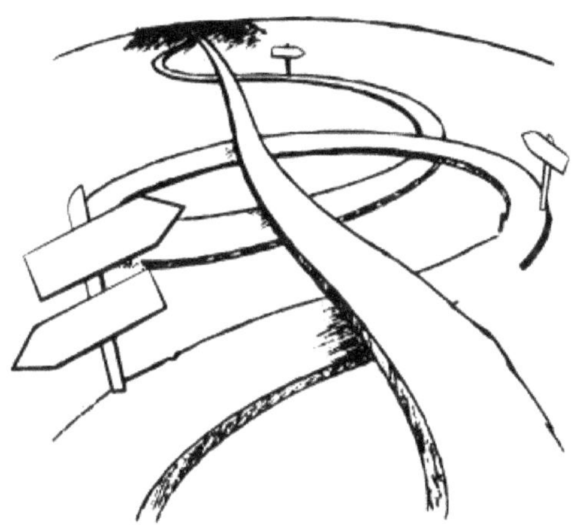